Bite Back II

Confessions of a Bed Bug Killer!

By Scott Linde, 25+ year Pest Expert

Published by:
SHL Enterprises
518-7 Old Post Road, Suite 181
Edison, N.J. 08817

ISBN: 978-0-9890110-0-6

TABLE OF CONTENTS

ABOUT SCOTT LINDE
aka P BUGGY

Scott Linde was born and raised in Brooklyn, N.Y. Mr. Linde started his career in pest control in 1988, working part-time. Since then, he has gone on to manage other pest companies for others and has owned and operated four pest-elimination and pest-control companies.

In 1992, Scott founded Staten Pesticide Consulting, a pesticide education company based in Staten Island, N.Y. He successfully taught over 200 individuals who went on to become licensed.

Mr. Linde continued teaching other exterminators when he moved out to New Jersey in 1998. Today, Mr. Linde is as passionate as ever about eliminating your household pests, particularly bed bugs.

SCHEDULE SCOTT aka P BUGGY TO SPEAK AT YOUR EVENT

If you are interested in booking P Buggy to speak, you can contact him at his office in Edison, N.J. P Buggy is available to speak nationally and internationally.

Today, Scott owns a pest control company that specializes in bed bug eradication. Throughout his career, P Buggy has owned four other pest companies and a pest consulting firm.

Scott was previously licensed by NYSDEC and NJDEP to give courses on pest-control laws and procedures.

His current pest company currently services the N.J. Tri-State area. If you are faced with bed bugs and would like to schedule a service, you can initially reach him at: PBuggy@bedbugkillers.com

If you are in his service area, he will be happy to assist you with your general insect and bed bug needs. Mr. Linde does not recommend other pest control companies unless he feels totally confident they can perform the job as well as he would. Currently, they are working on these relationships.

Stay tuned to :

http://www.BedBugKillers.com

as new information and new relationships emerge. Use this book as your hiring bible and ask the right questions before making any commitments.

P Buggy is an ideal Speaker for the following:

- Pest association meetings

- New small business start ups

- Strategies on bed bug prevention

- Private corporate meetings where bed bugs are a concern

Please contact P Buggy at 908-444-6097

By purchasing this book, I am happy to provide a 20 minute phone consultation for free (normally a $30 charge) provided you first do the following:

1. **You must go on Amazon and review this book.**

2. **You MUST forward me the receipt you receive on Amazon when you purchase the book.**

3. **Send me an email letting me know you have posted the review and send me the receipt.**

Share this Book with People You Care About, Help Me Help Them!

Empower and Equip Others!

Share This Book

How great would it be if you could help a friend, an associate or a loved one get through the trauma of Bed Bugs!

**Now you can, with my book
"Confessions of a Bed Bug Killer"**

In this book, P Buggy reveals street strategies that are easy to understand and apply. The goal of this book is to teach you how to effectively keep bed bugs out of your life.

Special Quantity Discounts

1- 20 Books	$15.00
21-99 Books	$14.00
100—499 Books	$13.00
500-999 Books	$12.00
1000+ Books	$11.00

(These discounts are **ONLY** available Directly though my website. They are not available through Amazon)

Prices do not include shipping. Shipping is extra.

* When you hire P Buggy to speak at your event, it comes with 100 books you can hand out to your captive audience.

This book is dedicated to everybody around the world who has ever been physically and emotionally bitten by bed bugs.

It's a freaking nightmare! And I hope this book gives you a clear understanding as to what is involved in eradicating bed bugs and helps you prevent new bed bug infestations.

Now It's Your Turn To... *Bite Back!*

Why I have earned the right to write my second book on Bed Bugs

Book ll is an update from Book l. While there will be some of the same information, I am presenting new facts based upon new experiences and research over the last 2 years. If you seem a little confused (I doubt it) as you read Book ll, then please purchase Book l. My name is Scott Linde aka P Buggy, and I'm a no B.S. type of guy. Born and raised in Brooklyn, New York, I was taught to give it to you straight, and that's EXACTLY what I intend to do.

I published my first book in November 2010 and it has become big hit all around the country. Since 2010 I have been exposed to new information I intend to share with you.

As an industry, we had no idea that in just a few years, bed bugs would be the dominant insect in the pest world.

On the web, on TV, on the radio all we hear about are bed bugs. It's even in sitcoms.

What's worse is the fact that a lot of manufacturers are taking advantage of you... the homeowner, by supplying chemicals and products that don't work against bed bugs — in some cases making things even worse because you have no clue what you need to do to use the product correctly. In New Jersey the DEP has even reached out to the EPA to have some of the current chemicals removed off the shelves because they do not work, based upon studies. However the EPA doesn't seem to want to be bothered so these useless products continue to be bought and used by Joe Public.

In recent education, we as a pest industry discovered that the initial chemicals we were using to kill bed bugs are now not killing bed bugs. What the Heck!

We as a pest industry have been trying to get a grip on this epidemic, but the EPA seems to make it harder and harder for us. In some states, politicians have even requested the EPA bring back products which we know worked against bed bugs in the past, but no luck! It's not only a fight against bed bugs, it's also a fight against the outside agencies and getting permission from them so we as an industry can do our job.

Don't get me wrong, the EPA is a valuable agency, we just want our chemicals back to fight against bed bugs.

I have also seen homeowners apply "bug bombs" in every room of their homes. I walked into one bedroom and almost passed out from the fumes a week after application. Bug bombs are the **WORST THING YOU CAN USE FOR BED BUGS!**

Personally I think it's funny when a homeowner sprays the shit out of their home with incorrect products and then has the gall to call us and ask if we use safe products (give me a break). We are licensed professionals and are guided by the EPA and state regulations on how we go about our treatments.

Now, as far as pest control companies go, not everyone is trained correctly or equally. Not every company is good, and not every company is bad! I believe that a pest control company is only as good as the technician it sends to do the job.

To get the most value out of this book, please read it in its entirety. I have not written it as a technical book with a lot of hard-to-understand words. I wrote this book to tell you what you need to know to help you get rid of your bed bugs. This book will save you time, money, and heartache.

Here is an email I just received last week. I had to make minor changes to protect this person but the entire email is true.

I had a very bad experience recently with a local New Jersey pest control company. I would like to forward you the document I wrote outlining the events (which I intend to send to the attorney general's office) but I'm not sure how secure the web is and am somewhat cautious about sending such info. via email.

I am a single XXXXXXX, not currently employed full time, working as a substitute teacher and going through a contentious divorce.

I have had several pest control companies come in and give me an estimate for using a thermal treatment to rid my home of the infestation. I would like to go this route as I have a special needs child and would really rather not use chemicals... Also, the prep involved for chemical treatments is beyond what I can handle since none of my friends or relatives will help as they are afraid of getting contaminated.

People will not visit me.

I have not seen any bugs since I got rid of my son's bed, encased all the mattresses and box springs, vacuumed and cleaned each bedroom.

Could I have eliminated the problem? I saw a live bug in my younger son's room and identified via the internet as a bed bug.

My son's bed had eggs and I saw a few live bugs.

I have tried calling several of the agencies that are child welfare agencies hoping to get some financial aid but they have offered me no help.

I called my Congressman... no help there.

What are lower income folks supposed to do?

Would it be safe for me to attach the aforementioned document?

Thank you.

I receive calls like that all the time. I wish I could smack all these guys providing this type of service but I can't. What I can do is educate you so it doesn't happen to you! I am on your side!

14

Disclaimer

The information provided in this book is designed to provide helpful information on the subjects discussed. This book is not meant to be used, nor should it be used, to diagnose or treat any medical condition. For diagnosis or treatment of any medical problem, consult your own physician. The publisher and author are not responsible for any specific health or allergy needs that may require medical supervision and are not liable for any damages or negative consequences from any treatment, action, application or preparation, to any person reading or following the information in this book. References are provided for informational purposes only and do not constitute endorsement of any websites or other sources. Readers should be aware that the websites listed in this book may change.

Language

This book is not intended for a young audience and should be kept out of range. On occasion the author will use strong language to emphasis a point. Based upon your culture you may or may not agree with the language being used. We encourage you to look for the points contained in the language.

Pictures

Pictures used in this book may seem somewhat graphic. Most are actual photos of our work in progress along with clients who agreed to have their pictures taken. No picture may be reproduced and/or used without the written consent of the author. Unauthorized use infringes on copyright laws.

QR Codes

Throughout this book I am going to display QR codes. This seems to be very common so you should be familiar with what they look like. The QR Codes will take you to some of my selected videos to gain a better understanding.

These are ONLY available on smart phones and by using a QR reader. QR readers are free in the app store on your smart phone. If you are old fashioned and not into this technology, not to worry. You won't be missing out on anything; you just won't have access to the data.

If you scan this QR code, you will receive a special message from me P Buggy.

Confession 1: Overview
Bed Bugs — What Are they, Why the Hell Are They Here in USA?

Quite honestly, unless you live under a rock, you have to have heard about bed bugs! They are on TV, in the news, etc. Actually they have become quite the celebrity.

Bedbugs are, literally, blood-suckers. They are an insect of the family Cimicidae that lives by hematophagy — feeding on the blood of humans and other warm-blooded hosts.

Adult bed bugs are reddish-brown, flattened, oval, and wingless, with microscopic hairs that give them a banded appearance. Newly hatched nymphs are translucent, lighter in color and become browner as they reach maturity. In size, they are often compared to lentils or apple seeds. Despite what most people think, they can be seen by the naked eye. Adults grow to 4-5 mm (1/8th to 3/16th of an inch) in length and do not move quickly enough to escape the notice of an attentive observer.

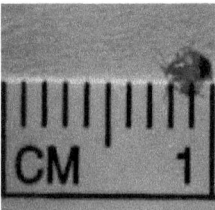

Some people believe you cannot see bed bugs. You most certainly can. This is a picture of an adult bed bug. The nymphs can also be seen.

Bed bugs live year-round and survive in most environments.

These small insects are nocturnal and prefer to live in places that have the closest access to their food source — YOU. They can live in or near a bed, box spring or headboards, or even in the furniture close to the bed. They want to be as close to the host — the human being — as possible. And depending on how severe the infestation is, they can also live in picture frames, behind lighting, and in carpets.

Although bed bugs can live for up to 5+ months without feeding (initially the research was 1 year), they normally try to feed every five to ten days. If there is a host present they are going to feed. Actually they MUST feed to survive.

Female bed bugs can lay up to five eggs in a day and 500 during a lifetime — an adult female can live up to two years.

Bedbug Life Cycle
4 Weeks - 5 Months Depending On Conditions

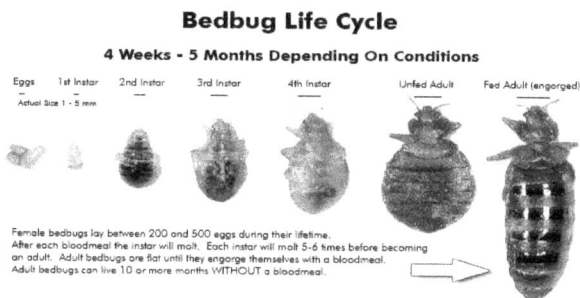

Eggs   1st Instar   2nd Instar   3rd Instar   4th Instar   Unfed Adult   Fed Adult (engorged)

Actual Size 1 - 5 mm

Female bedbugs lay between 200 and 500 eggs during their lifetime. After each bloodmeal the instar will molt. Each instar will molt 5-6 times before becoming an adult. Adult bedbugs are flat until they engorge themselves with a bloodmeal. Adult bedbugs can live 10 or more months WITHOUT a bloodmeal.

Bed bugs have to be introduced to a new environment, which often happens through hitch hiking on visiting guests, relatives, or even people putting backpacks or jackets near each other. It has nothing to do with being clean or being dirty, being rich or being poor.

The only difference is that the poor are sometimes not in a good enough financial position to properly deal with their bed bug infestations, so they can last longer.

Bed bugs are normally active just before dawn, with a peak feeding period about an hour before sunrise. However, they may attempt to feed at other times — given the opportunity — and have been observed to feed at any time of the day. In darker apartments and houses bed bugs may not be able to distinguish between night and day, causing rapid growth of infestation.

Each year Orkin releases a list of the top 15 most infested bed bug states. Here is their most recent update 2012. If you were to refer back to Book 1, you would see the states have changed. New York is no longer the king of the hill.

If you do a search on this you will be amazed as these Cities/States move up and down the charts. Which brings me back to this point; "no one is immune from getting Bed Bugs."

1. Cincinnati, OH
2. Chicago, IL
3. Detroit, MI
4. Denver, CO
5. Los Angeles, CA
6. Columbus, Ohio
7. Dallas Fort worth, Texas
8. Washington, DC
9. New York, NY
10. Richmond/ Petersburg, VA
11. Houston
12. San Frisco, CA
13. Cleveland, OH
14. Boston, MA
15. Dayton, Ohio

Confession 2: The Mind Fuck Bug

Bed bugs are not like any other bugs I have ever come across. People are so freaked out by bed bugs, even after the bugs have been eradicated, some still believe they feel as if they are getting bitten. We have some clients who can't believe the bed bugs are gone so they pay K-9 teams over and over to keep coming back to check their homes. Even after the K-9 team clears their home, some still believe something is there.

We had a gentleman in who became so freaked out, he believed every speck he found on his new sheet set was an indication of bed bugs. The guy is so mentally screwed up, he had to start seeing a shrink to calm down. When he calls me, he cries. Truly, I feel really bad for him. I try to ease his mind and put everything in perspective. He has spent a lot of money on covers, climb ups, new bed and even fumigation.

Now not everybody is this freaked out, but a lot are freaked out and will experience lack of sleep, panic attacks or just keep feeling they are getting bitten after the bugs are gone.

Please do yourself a favor by realizing that the mind is very powerful and may be presenting you with a situation that is not there. Don't get me wrong, sometimes there are baby bed bugs that still may be around causing havoc, but that is not always the case. Once again, let me emphasis, choose the pest company you hire cautiously.

I have a chapter later in this book that describes the top questions you should ask prior to hiring any pest company to treat for bed bugs.

Confession 3: The Bed Bug Battle

Battling bed bugs in your environment

Unfortunately, the problem isn't just limited to residential communities. Department stores have had to temporarily shut down, they have also been found in movie theaters, offices - you can't be so naïve as to think you will never get affected by bed bugs. It can happen to the best of us. No matter how careful you may be, all it takes is one rogue bed bug to fuck your world up! And I assure you, you would be fucked up!

How To Inspect For Bed Bugs In Public

Speaking of public places, it seems like no place is safe. I'm not trying to scare the crap out of you, but I also don't want you to be that naive that you just don't pay attention and think bed bugs will never happen to you. You did spend money on this book, so please don't be an idiot!

Movie Theaters
Here's what you need to do at the movies to avoid inadvertently becoming a target. This advice is particularly for the ladies, but it also applies to men who carry around bags or for people who are wearing coats.

Before you sit down, don't put your purse or jacket on the chair next to you. I recommend that you plan on keeping it in your lap for the entire time. Next, take out one of those mini flashlights or use the light from your phone (Who would have thought it would have come to this?) and inspect the crevices on the front of the seats for bed bugs. Inspect the seats next to you as well. These extra steps could help prevent you from bringing those bed bugs home from the movies.

Personally I am scared shitless every time we go to the movies. When we get home we all strip immediately and put EVERYTHING in the dryer on high heat.

I understand that these things may sound crazy, but they have to be done in these bed bug-infested times. Look, you don't have to listen to anything I say. Actually I hope you don't! It gives us, the pest extermination industry, an opportunity to make a shit load of money off your laziness.

Garage Sales and Consignment Shops

If you are one of those people who like to bargain shop at one of these placcs, make sure you inspect items for bed bugs, blood stains, or black specks, which could be bed bug feces. Remember that bed bugs like to hide in crevices and you may not detect them. As a result, you could come home with some things you didn't bargain for!

Used Furniture and Furniture Stores

I understand some of the current economic pressures you may face, between millions of people out of work and a current president who is bankrupting this county, it's just not easy. But I have to be direct with you. Please stay the heck away from used furniture! I find these types of purchases with section 8 and welfare tenants.

I can't tell you how many times these tenants have infested their apartments with these types of items.... and they will just blame the landlord! It happens all the time.

There are no savings when you bring home more than you ever expected. Listen, if you see furniture out on a curb, it's meant to be there, not in your house!

Just the other day, we went to treat an apartment in Perth Amboy, N.J. for bed bugs. The tenant tossed all their furniture in the back yard. There were hundreds of live Bed Bugs on the mattress and box spring. If a local person passes by and sees these items and takes it to make his very own, guess what????????

This Video is of the stuff in the back yard.

Department Stores

You know how some people buy clothes and return them after trying them on at home? Well, guess what? These people could have a bed bug infestation at home, and if they do that designer shirt could get infested if left lying around. Then when that shirt is returned to the store, the bed bugs that found a home on the shirt now infest the store and potentially the next person who purchases the shirt.

And the bad news is that bed bugs could infest your home if you buy clothes and fail to inspect the crevices for bed bugs.

When you are shopping at department stores, you have to be alert and inspect everything before bringing anything home. When you do bring it home, toss it in the dryer IMMEDIATELY on high heat for 40 minutes. Note: You can put dry clean clothes only in a dry dryer on high heat.
And that's not just limited to clothing. Bed bugs have also been found in shoes and luggage. They can hitch a ride in just about anything you carry into your home. Our online store carries luggage spray and other items you can purchase to safe guard yourself.

Work Place

Several years ago, we were called into a known clothing brand name corporation. They rented five floors in NYC; each floor was approximately 25000 square feet.

I have to tell you, for me it was a nightmare!

Not only did we find bed bugs in multiple areas, we also had to deal with all the female drama which was worse. I am not trying to be a chauvinist but these women really needed a shot of calmness.

"This one had bed bugs so I must have Bed Bugs." "OMG I found bed bugs in my house."

It was nonstop. On several occasions, the company paid us to have one of our K-9 teams inspect apartments for bed bugs due to sightings by female employees. At every single inspection, we did NOT find any bed bugs. It was always something else such as carpet beetles, centipedes, etc.

Nevertheless, it all started in this company when this one female employee came into work one day and said she had bed bugs in her home. They did, in fact, find a live bed bug in her jacket. To this day, I still can't figure out why people just don't seem to give a shit about infecting other people with their bed bugs?

Initially they called in this pest company. Two guys showed up with two cans of aerosol spray and proceeded to walk around the floor during off hours and spray in the air. I swear you just can't make this stupid stuff up! Of course those idiots were thrown out and we were brought in.

There was another case study in which this gentleman was infesting his office with bed bugs. After weeks of inspections and research, it was determined he was the cause.

Apparently, his dress shirt collar was all blood stained from bed bugs. To him it was no big deal, he didn't think he was doing anything wrong. If I were you, I would buy a plastic bin with a cover to keep my jacket and pocket book sealed inside throughout my work day. I definitely would not allow my outerwear to sit in a common area and mingle with other outerwear that may be infested.

I would also purchase from our on-line store Bed Bug natural spray and spray the chair I sit in every week. You can access our on-line store at http://www.bedbugkillers.com

If you do work in a large environment and you do hear of a bed bug infestation, keep your composure and your sanity. Follow the steps I have laid out in this book and you will be ok.

College Frat Houses

I live close to Rutgers in New Jersey. Most college kids are broke and are doing their best to make it through the years on a limited budget. At the end of each semester all their furniture gets put out on the street for the taking. It actually happens during the year also. The problem is bed bugs. These kids don't care, they think they are invincible. We have treated so many college frat houses for bed bug infestations. The kids do cooperate when they need treatments.

We have also treated a lot of private homes due to the fact the college kids introduced bed bugs into their parent's home. Kids can get bed bugs at frat parties just by sitting on the couches. Again, make sure the kids are taught to follow the dryer procedures as listed above so it becomes second nature.

Just a several months ago, I received a call from a frantic father. His daughter was scheduled to move into a frat house last September. However they notified him, the house had bed bugs. He immediately moved his daughter's belongings out and called us to treat what she had.

Summer Rentals

In August 2012, a father is on the way down to move his daughter out of her summer rental. They found out the place she is staying has bed bugs. When he arrives he is picking up her things and I am meeting him at the storage facility. We are going to treat all her items with Nuvan Pro-strips. All the items will be placed in sealed bags for a minimum of 2 weeks, we will then return to pick them up. The strips are a strong product. We don't sell them directly to the customer; we place all of our strips.

House Guests

You have no idea on how many homes we treat for bed bugs due to house guests. I have to be honest, it's mostly foreigners, I have come to realize some friends and family members really don't care about you and are not concerned about infesting your home.

If they did, why would they come over and not let you know? You think they don't know? **Hogwash!** They know, but they don't give a shit so they don't tell you, then they leave, and their bed bugs stay behind. We service hundreds of homes like that. Don't be afraid to offend someone and ask. In this epidemic you have the right to know! Listen, it's your choice, of course, but if you don't ask and your home becomes infested then you have nobody to blame but yourself.

Field Study:

I go into a home in Piscataway, N.J. The home has been invaded by bed bugs and has turned the homeowners' lives upside down. Their 14-year-old daughter had a friend come to sleep over. The daughter saw a bug crawl out of the friend's knapsack and let her mother know. Who knew three months later that bug she saw was a bed bug and their house would become infested.

Field Study:

Big home, well-kept in Somerset, N.J. The homeowners had a guest stay in a spare bedroom for a couple of weeks. The guest infested the home with bed bugs. Guest leaves, bed bugs stay.

Field Study:

We service a lot of apartments in our area who house IT guys. They are all foreigners who travel from place to place. Most of them come with one suitcase and end up sleeping on the floor in their bedrooms. Some IT guys share the same bedrooms. You want to talk about Bed Bug infestations; it would absolutely blow your mind. It seems to be the norm for them.

Here is a picture we took just last week. All the dark crap you are looking at on the bed is live bed bugs, eggs and fecal matter. The tenant sleeps on this each night. I told him we were tossing out the bed and we did. You had to see the wall paneling in this room, it was just as loaded. The ONLY concern he had was how quick he could go back to his bedroom.

Can you imagine sleeping on the floor on this bed loaded with Bed Bugs?

We see it quite often, nasty shit you ever seen. I really don't get it but then again how could most?

All the blackness you see around the seams is live Bed Bugs, Bed Bug crap and Bed Bug eggs.

We threw this mattress out the back door

If you are going to have visitors stay in your guest room, make sure you alert them about your concerns of infesting your home with bed bugs. If they care about you at all, they will understand.

These guests left some of their guests behind. NOT FAIR!

Assisted Living Facilities

Man what a challenge these type of places can be. I have an associate of mine who services several of these places in New York State. They got to the point where they have a separate storage shed. All new residents/patients are required to put all of the items they bring into this shed. Then all items are inspected for bed bug activity. We have actually found that a lot of old people get their bed bug infestations from their visiting nurses or home care attendants. My point is just be careful.

This is truly a battle, a battle between you and your bed bug infestation. It's not going to be an easy battle: They want to live, and you want them dead!

Everything wants to survive — it's something we all possess, bugs included. Your goal is to find the most successful means to eradicate them.

> **Unfortunately, what people think will work in getting rid of bed bugs and their success rate don't always match up!**

I have seen many consumers mistakenly believe they can eradicate bed bugs just like they would cockroaches and other common pests. That's simply not true! Bed Bugs are a totally different animal.

But the worst part about this particular bug is that it doesn't just feed on your body, which is bad enough. It can also seriously mess with your mind.

I am sorry to say some customers take years to recover mentally from a bed bug infestation. At this very moment I am writing from my hotel room in Las Vegas.

I am scared and was scared for two weeks prior to coming. Why? Because I handle thousands of bed bug jobs, and while most hotels take the appropriate actions to ensure the safety of their guests, what happens if the guest before me brought bed bugs from home into my room and they are still here? I think about this all the time, and before I check out I am going to inspect the mattress, box-spring and headboard. I already check my white sheets each morning for any signs of left-behind blood.

I would die if I brought bed bugs home! Now, if a roach, ant or field mouse invaded my house, so what? I would handle it and forget about it. bed bugs are a serious mind fuck!

Here is a picture of a hotel I did work on. As you can see, the bed bug infestation was found behind the headboard. When staying in a hotel, I frequently look behind this area. These are scary times — I can't chance infesting my house with bed bugs.

As I said before, the majority of clients who have experienced bed bug issues suffer mentally from them even after the bed bugs have been physically removed.

The good news is with the correct resources your current bed bug issue can be resolved and your peace of mind restored. The key word here is correct resources — not just resources.

Bed Bug Bites

Bed bugs reach their host by crawling or sometimes climbing walls to a ceiling and jumping down upon feeling a heat wave. Attracted by warmth and the presence of carbon dioxide, the bug pierces the skin of its host with two hollow tubes. With one tube it injects its saliva, which contains anticoagulants and anesthetics. With the other, it draws the blood of its host. After feeding for about five minutes, the bug returns to its hiding place without the victim even realizing he's just been attacked.

The bites cannot usually be felt until some minutes or hours later, as a dermatological reaction to the injected agents. The first indication of a bite usually comes from the desire to scratch the bite site. Low infestations may be difficult to detect, and it is not unusual for victim not to even realize they have bed bugs early on. Patterns of bites in a row or a cluster are typical, as the bed bugs may be disturbed while feeding. Bites may be found in a variety of places on the body.

In most observed cases, bites consist of a raised red bump or flat welt and are often accompanied by very intense itching. The red bump or welts are the result of an allergic reaction to the anesthetic contained in the bed bug's saliva, which is inserted into the blood of its victim.

Bed bug bites may appear indistinguishable from mosquito bites, though they tend to last for longer periods. Bites may not become immediately visible and can take up to nine days to appear. They tend to not have a red dot in the center — a characteristic of flea bites. However, like flea bites they tend toward a sequential pattern. Bites are often aligned three in a row, giving rise to the colloquialism "fleas bite in threes." This may be caused by the bed bug being disturbed while eating and relocating half an inch or so farther down the skin before resuming feeding. Alternatively, the bed bug could also have been repeatedly searching for a blood vein.

Field Study:
On September 17, 2010, I was treating a very heavily infested two family house in Piscataway, NJ. I decided to pick up a bed bug and let it crawl on me. While it was on my hand and palm I could not feel it. I only felt a slight tingle when it reached my arm hairs

Field Study:
On September 22, 2010, we arrived in Newark, N.J., by plane. My associate at that time was itchy and had bite marks on his wrist and leg. We could not confirm what caused it, but it was not there before.

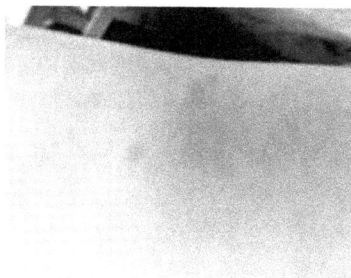

Here is a picture of my own arm with Bed Bug bites. I respond very quickly to bites and I break out. For me it's an itchy experience.

People react very differently to bed bugs, varying with skin type, environment, and the species of bug doing the biting. In some rare cases, allergic reactions to the bites may cause nausea and illness. In a large number of cases, about half of all people will show no visible sign of bites whatsoever, greatly increasing the difficulty of identifying and eradicating infestations.

People commonly react to bed bug infestations and their bites with anxiety, stress, and insomnia. Individuals may also get skin infections and scars from scratching the bite locations.

Most patients who are placed on systemic corticosteroids to treat the itching and burning often associated with bed bug bites find that the lesions are poorly responsive.

Antihistamines have been found to reduce itching in some cases, but they do not affect the appearance and duration of the lesions. Topical corticosteroids, such as hydrocortisone, have been reported to be effective at eliminating lesions and decreasing the associated itching.

According to an article in an issue in the New England Journal of Medicine dated September 4, 2008, topical corticosteroids were successfully used to treat a patient who was severely bitten by bed bugs. The patient had stayed in a hotel the night before and awoke to several reddish-brown bloodstains and flat insects on her bed. Her arms and breasts were covered with several lesions. The topical corticosteroids that were given to the patient completely resolved her symptoms within 2 days.

According to Dermatology: Diagnosis and Treatment, some patients may also experience temporary relief from itching and inflammation after applying hot water to the bite. The water should be quite hot (about 50 °C / 120 °F) because if it is not hot enough it may cause aggravation of the symptoms.

 It should be hot enough to cause minor discomfort, but care must be taken not to burn the skin. This treatment should only be self-administered in order to reduce that risk. Itching and inflammation can be relieved for several hours by applying hot running water, a hot washcloth, or even using a blow-dryer to heat the area of the bite, for 10 seconds to 1 minute (or longer if desired).

There is disagreement as to why heat causes the symptoms to abate. Some think heat overwhelms the nerve endings that signal itch. Others believe heat neutralizes the chemical that causes the inflammation, while still others think the heat triggers a large release of histamine causing a temporary histamine deficit in the area.

Bed bugs seem to possess all of the necessary prerequisites for being capable of passing diseases from one host to another. However, the good news is that there have been no known cases of this happening as of yet. There are at least 21 known pathogens (some estimates are as high as 41) that are capable of living inside a bed bug or on its mouthparts.

Extensive testing has been done in laboratory settings that also conclude that bed bugs are unlikely to pass disease from one person to another. Therefore, bedbugs are less dangerous than some more common insects such as the flea. However, transmission of Chagas disease or hepatitis B might be possible in appropriate settings.

Depending on your skin and blood chemistry, you may or may not feel a bite. People usually realize they've been bitten after noticing a couple of welts or red marks right next to each other.

Look for trickles of blood on pillows and sheets. A trickle of blood, if found with some staining, would indicate that a bed bug might have been feeding on you throughout the night. Bed bugs are nocturnal, so you're usually sleeping when they come out.

Watch this video as I allow bed bugs to crawl all over me and don't even............

Confession 4: How I Keep My Home Bed Bug Free

Travel/ Hotels
I travel all the time alone and with my family. My daughter also travels with the different groups she belongs to.

Up to now, we have not infested our home with bed bugs (Thank the lord). I used to get really nuts when traveling. I would actually work my way up into frenzy. There was one occasion I brought all my chemicals and equipment with us. I treated the entire hotel room while my wife and kids laughed at me. I'm admitting that I am scared. Throughout the years I have become more relaxed while traveling, but my guard is always up and that's why I don't have bed bugs.

 I am going to share with you EXACTLY what I do. It's up to you if you would like to follow my routine or not. Remember your laziness is our profit!

*** Hotels, especially the chains; work very hard with their staff to keep bed bugs out. What cannot be helped is when a guest checks in with bed bugs that then infests the room. The majority of places you will stay in will not create an issue for you. I am completing this chapter from Mexico, while traveling on vacation with my family. The first thing I did was ask the bellhop if they have bed bugs here?

He let me know about the property's procedure when it came to bed bug protection. So far, so good because there are no rashes, no bite marks and no blood spots on our sheets.

At the hotel:

A. When I check in, I ask the counter person if they are aware of any bed bugs in the hotel, and I watch for the reaction.

B. When I go into the room, I put my suitcase on the bed, not the luggage rack.

C. I turn on all the lights, and I pull the sheets back from the head board area.

D. I then pull the mattress out a little and I examine the ridge on the mattress for any black spots.

E. I then have access to the box-spring, so I pull it away from the bed or I lift it up a little looking for spots for activity.

F. If I am OK at this point, I put my clothes away and put my luggage in the closet or near the door.

G. Each morning when I get up, I check the white sheets for any blood staining.

H. When I go into the bathroom, I get naked and examine my body for any new rashes or marks. It's not a pretty sight but I must do it.

I. The day I am leaving I pull off all the sheets, lift up the bed all the way and examine underneath (sometimes it's heavy, but I do it)

J. I pull up the box-spring(s), and if it's a king bed there are two. I examine front, back, and sides. Then I put everything back, not neatly. (You think I'm extreme? Well, up to now I have not had any bed bugs in our home.)

When I arrive home:

A. I take the entire suitcase straight to the laundry room.

B. I take out all my dry cleaning and put it in sealed bag.

C. My wife washes everything regardless.

D. I inspect my toiletries and put them away.

E. I treat my entire suitcase with Steri-Fab, soaking it down.

F. I take a shower and put all my clothes in the wash.

This is how I do it and this is why we never bring bed bugs home! Thank GOODNESS!

**** We NEVER skip this step! We are not going to be lazy and infest our home with bed bugs.

In this video, I was staying at a hotel. I woke up in the morning with a bite mark on me I did not have the night before. Watch the video to see how I handle it.

Confession 5: What does the doctor know?

Field Study:
About four years ago, I received a call from a nearby resident. Her children and grandchildren just moved back from Israel, and she was concerned because her grandson had a bite mark on his face.

When I arrived, I started out by having a detailed conversation. The wife said she took her son to the dermatologist, who felt it was a flea bite. After doing a careful inspection I found the remains of bed bugs in a couple of the beds. I proposed a solution, which started with using our mattress covers. I told the mother I did in fact find bed bugs — not fleas — and asked the name of the doctor who misdiagnosed the problem. Now, get this: She said it was her father, who lived in the same house. I asked her why he would suggest fleas when the family didn't have any outside animals and the house wasn't having problems with strays.

She didn't seem to have a clue! Most people don't.

Field Study:
Just a while before writing this, we received a call from a furniture store in upstate New York. They had sold furniture to a couple, and the man of the house called the furniture store suggesting they sold them furniture with bed bugs. We were called to go in to inspect. I reached out to one of the several K-9 teams we use to go investigate and get back to

me. I received a call later that day to indicate the house was free of bed bugs. The homeowner told our K-9 team his nine-year-old daughter had been sleeping on her stomach and had signs of rashes. Yet when the parents went to the doctor to get her examined, the doctor told them they looked like bed bug marks.

<u>This is just two of many cases in which the doctors misdiagnosed bed bugs.</u> Now, I admit to not being a doctor, but from what I have heard most of them don't have a clue when it comes to bite marks on bodies — yet they are eager to diagnose.

I am happy to take clients' money when they call my office saying they have bed bugs because the doctor told them so. However, I need to be sure for myself prior to performing any treatment because I want to make sure I present them with the correct solution.

Confession 6: How To Inspect For Bed Bugs
Inspecting for Bedbugs

The following information can be used to inspect your residence for bed bugs. However, in some cases you may not be able to detect an infestation. If you cannot directly find evidence of bed bugs, the next step is to call in a professional pest company. I will discuss some smart questions that you should ask that company in a later chapter.

They're not social and they don't work in coordination with each other. However, because they emit a pheromone, bed bugs will usually end up together and remain in clumps. But sometimes that's not always the case. Sometimes it takes just one bed bug getting into your luggage to have an outbreak.

Usually, the outbreak will happen anywhere between four and six weeks after your residence becomes infested. We may go into a home and find adult bed bugs. If this is the case, then they have just been brought in. At this point, you need to act very quickly so as to minimize the infestation.

The Mattress
Remove your sheets and bed protector from your mattress. Take your finger and run it along the edge of the bed and look for any kind of black or red staining. Pull the mattress back off of the box-spring. Look on the seams underneath your mattress (the side that was lying right on top of the box-spring) for staining or bugs. You'll be able to see bed bugs

with the naked eye. If you do see bed bugs, you can do the following right away:

1. <u>Vacuum this area of the mattress</u>. You must throw out the bag afterwards. If you use a bagless vacuum, make sure to thoroughly wash out the container.

2. Spray the infested area with straight rubbing alcohol. This will immediately kill the live bed bugs. Once the alcohol dries the effect of killing is gone. If you use this method make sure to wear eye protection and open the windows for proper ventilation.

Use this method at your own discretion; the author is not responsible for how you decide to apply this application.

This is the part where most people lose their minds and do all kinds of crazy stuff!

Note: some mattresses have vent holes throughout. Bed bugs may be living inside the mattress. In these cases, you will not see the bed bugs.

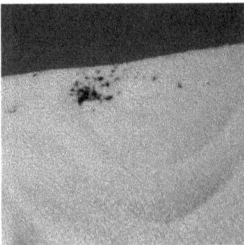

Some people still believe bed bugs cannot be seen, but this mattress has visible evidence of a bed bug infestation. As you can see for yourself, the cluster is easily detected. Our client thought he fixed his problem himself, until I showed him his box-spring.

The Box-Spring

Bed bugs are also commonly found in or on the box-spring. Box-springs are less disturbed by humans and create the ideal hiding place for an infestation. Once the mattress is taken off the box-spring, you will need to stand the box-spring straight up. The head board side should be up in the air. Take your finger and run it along the seams of the box-spring. If you find black marks, these are the feces of the bed bugs. You may even find red marks. Bed bugs will congregate together.

1. If you have corner pieces on your box-spring, you will need to pull them back to look underneath.

2. The black felt cover on the box-spring will need to be slowly removed, starting from the top. This is a hot spot for bed bugs, so be ready to act with your vacuum and alcohol spray. The black felt can be removed and thrown away. It has nothing to do with the integrity of the box-spring.

Note: If you use rubbing alcohol, make sure you do not get any on either your wood floors or your wood furniture. Also, protect your face and eyes. Make sure to open a window, as the alcohol will have a strong odor and may affect you.

**Box Springs MUST be examined!
VERY IMPORTANT!**

Steri-Fab is a quick bed bug kill product. You must use caution when using it because it is very strong. You can find this product on our website under "store"

This is an apartment bedroom we were called in to inspect and treat for bed bugs. The person had clutter everywhere. We found a big infestation of bed bugs on both box- springs always *use two techs initially.*

The headboard and bed frame

I personally have been finding wooden headboards to be somewhat of a challenge. On several occasions, we could not eliminate the infestations until we had the clients throw out their bed frame or wrap them and take them out of the structure. Wood is very porous, and no matter how hard we treat it, the treatment doesn't always perform as well as I need it to, so the headboard must be removed.

HOWEVER, since we incorporated heat treatments into our bed bug eradication process, we have seen better results. We have recently incorporated the Nuvan Pro Strips and have also achieved great results.

When I mentioned products we use, we are highly trained to use them. All chemical treatments should be left to the professionals.

The furniture

It is not uncommon for us to find bed bugs in the nearby furniture. It really depends on the level of infestation. Your bed frame, your dressers, nightstands and nearby pictures may also be infested. I know it sounds very scary, but the truth of the matter is the longer you wait to have your home treated the bigger the bed bug infestation grows and the larger the area of infestation.

If you have already started to self-treat, you will likely find clusters of bed bugs behind picture frames, wall moldings, under night lamps, etc.

If you use the wrong chemicals (which you will)...

YOU ARE GOING TO MAKE MATTERS WORSE

Some people believe that only dirty people have bed bugs. This is NOT the case. We service multi-million dollar homes on a regular basis. These homes are far from dirty. Bed bugs are not after dirt — you are the meal!

The couch

The couch is another hot spot for bed bug infestations. Bed bugs are transferred from one area to the next by clothes. If you have bed bugs on your pajamas, boxers, suit pants, etc., there is a good chance you are going to infest other areas of your home just by staying in these other areas. Sleeping on an infested mattress, and then waking up to watch TV on the couch could infest the couch and the couch area because bed bugs will crawl off your pajamas when you sit down.

Here we moved the bottom of the couch. The dog altered us to bed bugs, and we are on a mission to seek and destroy! As you see, we take our business seriously.

If the company you hire does not treat with this intensity, DON'T HIRE THEM!!!

I am going to emphasize a point here: You are reading this book to become educated. If you have a bed bug issue and are calling for service NEVER start the conversation by asking, "How much do you charge to get rid of bed bugs?"

Sorry, it's a dumb question. You want to know what their procedures and warranties are first. Then, get them to come out and take a look. Only after that happens should you discuss price.

The Dos and Don'ts of Handling Your Bed Bug Problems

Actions to take if you find bed bugs:
As I already said, if you find bed bugs somewhere in your home, there is a high possibility that there may be additional areas of infestation throughout your home — even if you don't see them or think they are there.

Field Study:
On February 15, 2010, we visited a new house in Monroe Township, N.J. The homeowners believed the bed bugs were just in their bedroom. During our inspection, we found live bed bugs under their couch in their living room on their main floor. The homeowners had no idea they were there.
At this point, remain calm and start an eradication procedure. This is going to consist of several steps.

Get PROFESSIONAL mattress and box-spring covers. You will also find an instruction sheet on how to measure your bed on our website. Order covers for both mattress and box-springs for every bed on the premises.

Here is a job we did in which we placed our covers on the bed. As you can see by the picture, the covers are properly fitted to the bed.

Having the **CORRECT** covers on the mattress and box-spring makes a world of difference.

While there are a lot of covers on the market — from cheap plastic to fancier material — the Protect-A-Bed brand has the covers I feel most comfortable using since they have been tested and proven by entomologists to work, thanks to their zippers and the bed bug lock-out method they use. I also prefer these covers because they are "fitted" and not just one size fits all. These are our main covers we use with each job. I am not paid to make this statement. I have a lot of confidence in the product and in its ability to perform to the level I need it to for our customers. Please don't be silly, a cheap plastic cover marked "Bed Bugs" will not work.
Spend the right money to get the right product.

Field Study:
A lot of bed cover manufacturers have now added the label "Bed bugs and dust mites." That's bull crap! A cheap plastic oversized cover you buy in the store or on the Internet is NOT going to do anything but take your money.

1. We have been in several homes where cheap covers consisted of paper-thin plastic that ripped to the

touch. I don't care what the label promises — it's not going to work. **Crap is crap!**

2. Over-sized or "one size fits all" covers are garbage. They create pockets and areas for bed bugs to hide. The entire purpose of the cover is to be able to properly inspect it. Don't buy oversized covers. It isn't going to work!

3. Cheap zippers and the teeth that lock the zipper will allow bed bugs to easily enter and leave.

Field Study:

We were servicing an apartment in Newark, N.J. In one of our buildings, the tenants refused to take our advice, and the husband (being hard-headed) purchased covers from the store. The wife kept complaining about bed bugs. When I examined her bed and cover, I found hundreds of bed bugs going in and out of the teeth of the zipper. I showed her, and of course the drama started. I let her know the longer she kept fighting, the more issues they would have. And they were inadvertently infesting the other tenants too.

Field Study:

We had another customer who agreed to purchase our covers for some of their beds. The remaining beds would receive covers from elsewhere. When we went back, the covers they purchased on their own were NOT the right fit. One bed was 9 feet long, and they had a 14 foot cover on the bed. Again, the "one size fits all" cover and the incorrect zipper mechanism WILL NOT give you the protection needed. I showed this customer that with the discount we gave her, she could have the right covers for cheaper than the wrong ones. She took my advice, and it all worked out.

Another customer bought a store cover. It had several rips, and one part was being held together with a pin. The cover was junk and doing nothing. If you bring in pest control companies, and they tell you to go pick up any bed cover from the store, **THROW THEM OUT OF YOUR HOUSE!** This is a clear indication that they are untrained and chances are their treatment will NOT work out for you.

The reality is that major retailers (both offline and online) stock items such as 'Bed Bug covers' that may make false claims. To them, it really doesn't matter whether the product works or not. They are not there to educate you on the product or take responsibility for it because it's not theirs. These covers have not been tested, and they simply won't do the job.

Field Study:

On Sept. 17, 2010, we were treating a two-family house for bed bugs. The owner of the house bought a box of covers marked "Bed Bugs and Dust Mites." **TOTAL JUNK.** They were paper-thin. I can understand his frustration, as he said he had been battling bed bugs with tenants for three years now. At best he was hoping to keep the infestation down to a minimum. The tenant upstairs paid us directly to order the proper covers for him and his family.

I also see this frequently in rentals. Most tenants are broke, so they go buy crap. Covers that are paper thin and tear to the touch. Here is a homemade cover we just came across last week. Talk about some redneck shit. (LMAO!)

My son is holding up a homemade Bed Bug cover. Needless to say, the cover was all ripped underneath. And the tenant is still getting bitten. Do you see what can happen when you go the cheap route?

Field Study:

The picture you see above was taken in a 14 unit building. 13 out of the 14 units had signs of bed bugs both heavy and light infestations. The landlord has had several pest control companies in the past service this property.

According to the tenants, the companies sucked and the landlord was cheap and would not pay to have it done correctly. A lot of the tenants called my office up wanting a copy of our report of findings. I let them know it was confidential.

Here's a photo of yours truly! We had just gotten done applying a residual dust called Drione Insecticide, and I had just finished installing *Protect-A-Bed* Covers. These covers were installed on every mattress and box-spring in the apartment. The landlord flipped the bill.

Call a qualified pest company in your area. I am going to emphasize **QUALIFIED**.

Bed bugs are a fairly new insect to most companies. Just because a pest company or pest technician may be good at killing general pests, it does not mean they are qualified to help you with bed bugs.

To "Bite Back" visit our website and order the proper covers at: http://www.bedbugkillers.com
Start to remove your clothes and articles from the infested area.

All clothes, shoes, pocketbooks, etc., need to be isolated immediately. Clothes should be washed in very hot water and then placed in the dryer on high heat. For clothes that need to be dry-cleaned, put these clothes directly in the dryer on high heat for about 45 minutes. This will kill bed bugs throughout their life cycle.

You can then give the clothes over to the dry cleaner for

further cleaning. A dry cleaning machine uses high heat to dry your clothes after they are washed in the dry cleaning machine. It is part of the same machine and the last phase before your clothes come out and get turned over to the presser.

Treating luggage at home
First, wash all of your laundry items in very hot water and put them in the dryer. The hot water and the dryer will kill the eggs. **Very high heat, Cryonite or fumigation is the only thing that will kill the eggs, not chemicals.**

Put everything in the dryer, including sneakers, shoes, and boots. To clean your luggage, you can purchase something called *Steri-fab*. *Steri-fab* is an alcohol-based chemical that acts as a bactericide and a fungicide and will also readily kill bed bugs.

It's a very strong alcohol-based product. So when using this product you have to make sure the windows are open and the kids are out of the way. You can also pick up some rubbing alcohol. Rubbing alcohol and steri-fab use the same base product, namely alcohol. You can put it in a spray bottle and spray it around your luggage for immediate results. If you are carrying around bed bugs and they are in your luggage, applying this product will instantly wipe the bed bugs out.

For sensitive articles, I recommend using the "**Packtite**" unit. You can find out more about this product on our website, http//www.bedbugkillers.com

Actions you should NOT take if you find bed bugs:

> **Do not pick up store-bought products and start spraying, EVER!**

This is not an effective method. Chances are you are not going to apply these products correctly. You may even cause the current infestation to move into other areas, including adjacent structures.

I have to admit I have seen some crazy things people do to handle infestations. There is a product on the market called DE or Diatomaceous Earth. This is considered a "green product." I have seen homeowners place this product all around their floor and even on their bed where they sleep.

Just because a product is "green" doesn't mean it can be thrown around like a yarn of string.

All pesticides green or not, require caution and the correct application procedures when using them. Failure to comply with the pesticide label is a violation of the instructions and may cause harm to you and/or your family and pets.

This is a picture of me pulling up the fabric on the same box-spring. As you can see even with his treatment, there is still a large cluster of bed bugs. These bed bugs have been feeding on him each night. What's worse is his landlord doesn't seem to care.

The tenant could not believe what he was looking at. He thought he did a great job

Field Study:

A homeowner in South River, N.J., finds bed bugs in his bedroom. He immediately goes on the Internet and purchases do-it-yourself products.

He picks up a spray and a dust marked for bed bugs and takes the dust and sprinkles it all over his box-spring. He then sleeps on it. (It's worse than the picture I have prior to this page.) Now think about this: Every time he lies down or gets up his bed bounces and, whether he knows it or not, the dust particles are being released into the air and he and his loved ones are breathing them in. Not only that, but guess what?

IT'S NOT DOING ANYTHING TO GET RID OF THE BED BUGS.

Field Study:
The same thing also happened in Monroe, N.J. Parents sprinkled bug dust they bought on the Internet on the wooden frame of their daughter's bed —inadvertently poisoning their daughter!

Do not throw out your mattress and/or box-spring. Sometimes people get very panicky, and they wind up throwing out their beds and mattresses. This is not correct for several reasons:

1. Mattresses and box-springs will be dragged through the other areas, causing the bed bugs to fall off the beds and onto the carpets and floors in additional areas. As a result, there will be more areas of infestation.

2. Just because the beds are thrown out, don't think the infestation is gone. While initially you may find relief and think the problem is gone, the bed bugs that got left behind will regroup, and in a short time you will be dealing with the same level of infestation.

> **The bottom line is that you could end up infecting other parts of your home when you do this, and it won't guarantee you will get rid of all your bed bugs.**

I had a woman who came to clean my house tell me about her daughter who had a bed bug problem. Well, her daughter decided to throw out a grand piano, major artwork, and the furniture. She basically emptied the apartment. So I asked the lady, "Ma'am, I'm not saying this to be funny or rude, but is your daughter stupid?" She replied, "No. My daughter has a PhD."

I said, "That's not what I asked. Is your daughter stupid? Why would she possibly get rid of all these items?" She said, "Well, the exterminator told her to do it." To put it bluntly, some exterminator companies send out knuckleheads to perform work. If an exterminator gives you advice that sounds crazy to you, go get a second opinion because clearly that is not the right guy to fix your problem.

Funny thing, though, is that the woman calls me in August 2010 and says, "My daughter has bed bugs again in their new home." They did not get it from their stuff because they got rid of EVERYTHING prior to moving into their new home. They had a guest come over and stay in one of their bedrooms, and now they have bed bugs. Since then she has moved twice and has gotten bed bugs in each house she moved into. She spends a lot of money with us; we fix her issues each time.

Since we met with her, we brought in our K-9 bed bug team. The dogs alerted us to infestations in three rooms. We decided to treat these areas with heat. We had our K-9 follow up scheduled for the following Wednesday.

The dog went and confirmed: **NO MORE BED BUGS!**

We were servicing one of our six family houses in Elizabeth, N.J, and found three mattresses outside. Nobody just throws out their mattress, so it was a good indication something was going on. Upon careful inspection, I found live bed bugs on the mattress. The problem is somebody is going to come along and take this mattress home. They are going to infest their apartment and then blame the landlord for having bed bugs

Do not set off bug bombs. This is a **VERY** bad idea and will not help you. Bug bombs are made for small flies and cockroaches. Setting off bug bombs is going to make matters worse because the bed bugs will crawl into wall voids to hide.

NO BUG BOMBS

My advice is to leave the pesticides to the professionals. A certified pest applicator spends numerous hours in classrooms and field training. Each state requires a series of written tests that an individual must pass to become certified in that state.

It can take up to two years of training before the state issues a license to apply pesticides. Not all technicians are certified because they are allowed to work under the company's license. The company is responsible for all applications made by the unlicensed technician.

In a later chapter, I am going to give you clear-cut advice on what to look for when interviewing a pest control company in your area.

> **Tenants seem to set off bug bombs a LOT. A landlord should never allow this, as the tenant has an opportunity to infest the neighbors' apartments.**

**It truly is a bomb!
Supers are notorious for
setting off bombs**

Confession 7: Bed Bug Methods

Bed Bug treatments are not cheap and should not be approached with an eye solely toward cost because one thing is certain: **Cheap is cheap**, and a low-bidding pest control company isn't going to give you the results you are after. I had an Egyptian customer say to me one time that "cheap is expensive and expensive is cheap." I agree completely. I own my own home, and life's little mishaps always seem to occur when I'm least financially prepared. However, if I need to fix something I believe in fixing it right the first time.

I receive a lot of calls from shoppers asking me questions I cannot possibly answer unless I pay them a visit. They have this cheap mentality and honestly it's a waste of my time. Let them find the cheapest price and get serviced by somebody else.

<u>I am sorry to inform you that not all pest control companies operate the same way when it comes to bed bugs.</u> You can talk to 10 different pest companies and come away with so many conflicting answers that it will leave your head spinning. I was taught a long time ago from a supervisor that it's not the company you actually hire that is going to determine your outcome — it is the skill of the technician that is going to fix any pest issue you have. The bigger the company you call the less opportunity you are going to have to deal with the owner or upper management.

It's been my experience that the overwhelming majority of

bed bug exterminators use both chemical and non-chemical approaches. There is no way around chemicals if you are looking for long-term results. They must be used for residual purposes. Up to this date, I have personally done over 3000 bed bug applications. I consistently attend classes, consult with entomologists and incorporate new procedures into my company. If I could save my chemical costs and do bed bug jobs without chemicals I would, but it is just not as effective. Heat & Fumigation require no chemicals.

Here is a list of some of the Bed Bug procedures you may see being offered:

1. **Cryonite** (freezing method) — This is a non-chemical approach and will kill all stages of bed bugs it hits directly. It works well as long as it directly comes in contact with the bed bugs when applied. It's a good selling product for those who just don't want to use pesticides. The trouble is it doesn't work well as a stand-alone. What if the bed bugs are out of range or in the wall voids during an application? This method will do nothing to stop an on-going infestation and is only used as a spot application. Once the service is over, the service is over! If you live in an apartment and your neighbors have bed bugs, this method may not produce the proper results, and you may become infested with bed bugs too. We incorporate Cryonite in our applications as needed.

2. **Steam** — We use high-heated steamers as part of our services. Like freezing, heating will destroy all stages of bed bugs. Again, this is only the case if we actually hit the bed bugs when steaming. In a lot of cases, I find that wooden bed frames pose a challenge. In hard-to-correct cases we implement hot steam when treating the wooden bed frames. We dissemble the entire frame and steam each area. Once completed, we then re-apply pesticides. Notice that we are not just applying the steam — we must apply a pesticide also. We need to create a residual barrier that will continue to kill bed bugs.

3. **High levels of heat** (we work with this very effective technology a lot) — some companies, including mine, offer an entire house/apartment heating. They have huge generators that feed heating and fan lines into the structure. They heat the structure up to 140 degree for a period of four to six hours. This method will kill all stages of bed bugs, providing the treatment is done correctly and it comes in contact with the bed bugs. The more clutter a structure has the less likely it is that the application will work. This procedure can cost you $1,600 or more per application. Again, once the heating is completed you still have no barrier in place for the bed bugs that were missed, but this is a

specialty application: The equipment is very expensive and the results are amazing.

This is a photo of my company setting up our heat treatment in a high-end home. We also incorporated a residual treatment and a K-9 follow up. I gave these people an option for treatment: Conventional or heat. They went with the heat, so I included the conventional and the dog follow up.

More photos of us using heat treatment for our customers. While we do conventional bed bug treatments, most like the fact that we can eliminate all their bed bugs in the same day. For them it eliminates embarrassment.

If you are in the New Jersey tri-state area, just call my office at (908) 444-6097 to discuss how our heat treatment can best work for you. Call my office to **"BITE BACK."**

The use of heat to kill bed bugs goes as far back as the 1960s. However, it didn't start to gain widespread use until about 10 years ago. Bed bugs have not demonstrated any signs of resistance to heat treatment thus far.

Hopefully, they never will!

Our company uses heating equipment, and both our customers and our team have been pleased with the results. If you're a pest control company and would like to find out more about heat treatment just visit: http://bedbugkillers.com

4. **Fumigation** — This can only be done by a licensed fumigation company. In single-family detached homes the entire house can be prepared and fumigated. The gas will penetrate all areas — such as furniture, walls, clothing, etc. — and kill everything in the house. The home must be vacant for 24 hours before re-entry. In attached homes or apartment buildings, fumigation can only be used by removing all furniture, clothes, etc., into a boxed area and fumigating the items outside the structure. The structure itself still needs to be treated using conventional pest-control methods. This is a very complicated process and takes several companies to get the job done. But fumigation can be fiercely effective because **it will kill EVERYTHING** the gas comes in contact with, and no prep is needed.

5. **Insect Interceptors** — These devices are used to make bed bug monitoring easy for you. An insect interceptor is a plastic, double well cup that has a slick, talc-coated interior. The exterior is fiber-coated. All you have to do

is place one of these devices under the leg of furniture where humans or pets sleep. These devices take advantage of the natural behavior of bed bugs to search for human hosts and their tendency to climb vertical coarse surfaces. Once bed bugs crawl into an interceptor, they are trapped because they can't crawl up the slick, coated interior wall. At the back of the book, there is an order form that will allow you to receive a discount for getting insect interceptors for your home.

Here is a picture of one of many insect interceptors. These can be washed and re-powdered fight against bed bugs.

Up to date they now make so many different monitors it can make your head spin. I recently saw a new glue monitor come out. Their fake claim is Bed bugs are attracted to it.

BULLSHIT! Yes, bed bugs will go into the trap if they are traveling in that vicinity but the product offers nothing but glue.

6. **Pesticides** – Pesticides are part of the bed bug eradication process. There are standard and 'green pesticides'.

Other chemical options

Some bed bug exterminators use a combination of cedar oil, along with other oils and heat, to kill bed bugs. Cedar oil can kill bed bugs only if it's directly applied to them. Others use a substance called Diatomaceous Earth.

Diatomaceous Earth (DE), also known as diatomite or kieselgur, is a naturally occurring, soft, siliceous sedimentary rock that is easily crumbled into a fine white to off-white powder. It has a particle size ranging from less than 1 micron to more than 1 mm, but typically 10 to 200 microns. This powder has an abrasive feel and is very light, due to its high porosity.

Diatomaceous Earth is considered a 'green' pesticide. DE can kill bed bugs because it absorbs lipids from the waxy outer layer of insects' exoskeletons, causing them to dehydrate. However, the product has some drawbacks.

First, it works slowly. It can take several days for bed bugs to dehydrate to the point where they die. Other pesticides can kill bed bugs in as little as one hour.

Second, applying DE is very tricky because it requires an extremely fine dusting. The average consumer does not possess the expertise to do it correctly. Moreover, applicators are not readily available to consumers.

Furthermore, Diatomaceous Earth also carries with it health risks. The absorbent qualities of diatomite can result in a significant drying of the hands if handled without gloves. The flux-calcined form contains a highly crystalline form of silica, resulting in sharp edges. The sharpness of this version of the material makes it **dangerous** to breathe and a dust mask is recommended when working with it.

The type of hazard posed by inhalation depends on the form of the silica. Crystalline silica poses a serious inhalation hazard because it can cause silicosis. Amorphous silica can cause dusty lungs, but does not carry the same degree of risk as crystalline silica. Natural or dried diatomite generally contains very low amounts of crystalline silica.

The crystalline silica content of the particulate dusts is regulated in the United States by the Occupational Safety and Health Administration (OSHA), and there are guidelines for the maximum amounts allowable in the product and in the air.

Pyrethroids are no longer as effective for killing Bed Bugs.

Initially the products we had available to kill bed bugs were Pyrethoid based; similar to what you find in many bug bombs and over the counter sprays. This is no longer the case. This is why I encourage you NOT to use over the counter sprays. Not only are the products you buy ineffective, in most cases, they are going to make matters worse by pushing the bed bugs into other areas. Bed bugs seem to becoming more and more resistant to pesticides.

Introduction of Bull Shit Products

In my opinion thieves come in many different shapes and sizes. I now find them to be in the shape of a pesticide product you find in your local hardware store or the shape of a cheap mattress cover you find in your local bedding or department store.

I think it's a damn shame these manufacturers are allowed to make false claims and get away with it. They are making billions of dollars preying on the fears of others.

Listen, really listen to this: Those products don't effin work (for those of you who don't understand (Effin = fucking)

You say "well how can they be on the shelves?" And my rebuttal to you is...they are and you are being scammed. You're just another sucker feeding the financial pipeline.

I get hundreds of calls from potential customers who say "I bought all these products and it won't fix my issue." No shit Sherlock, every media station tells you to seek professional pest control for bed bug infestations.

Like I said, spray away, spend your money and then when you're ready call and hire a professional company.

Some Final Thoughts On Pesticides
I attend a lot of classes on bed bugs and listen to a lot of entomologists. Do yourself a favor and leave the chemical applications to the experts. I am going to emphasize the word **experts**. Your neighbor, the guy selling bed bug products on the internet, your best friend or the floor person working at the large home improvement store is NOT an

expert.

If you do additional research, you will find that a combination of different products and services is what will eventually eradicate your infestation. There is no single procedure or product that will work.

Confession 8: That Bitch May Not Be Right - Canine Inspections

I remember when I first got introduced to a K-9 who worked with a handler and sniffed out bed bugs. This client we had kept complaining that her bed bug issue was not being resolved.

I told her there was nothing here but she insisted. We brought in our 1st K-9 team who went through each room sniffing away. The K-9 cleared the house and I was very happy.

I let her know "we were done" I told her whatever was happening to her was not the result of bed bugs and she should go see a doctor. It turns out she had mold in her basement and since she was allergic to mold she was breaking out.

I have had several cases like this. I have one woman now who calls my office three times a month insisting she has bed bugs. I send the dog, she has no bed bugs and she feels relieved and I make money. It's a happy relationship all around.

Throughout the years, I have come across some really good handlers and some really bad ones. I have worked with handlers who miss an entire infestation. I fire them immediately.

Look it's like anything else. Companies may start off producing a good product but then they become greedy so they mass produce and give up quality. K-9's and handlers buy from these companies.

I don't work with inexperienced handlers. What I have come across is people who lose their jobs so instead of being life coaches which used to be the norm, they now go out spend 10K on getting trained as a Bed Bug K-9 inspector and start marketing themselves as experts.

You have a right to ask the handler about what type of experience he has and what kind of training his dog has.

K-9's are **NOT all the same** and the results are not always the same. Like anything else, you must take time to do the proper research. Otherwise the money you spend to bring in a K-9 goes down the drain.

Ask to see the certification and training log. If they can't/won't produce what you need, don't use them.

CASE STUDY: I recently received a call from a woman in NJ. She had used a few different

K-9 handlers to seek out bed bugs in her house. Some dogs alerted to the same areas and some dogs missed an entire area.

The last dog she used was not certified. She knew it. I asked her why she would do that. Her reply was "I don't have the money to keep bringing in certified dogs."

So the woman pays for a bullshit dog with no certification and likes the results because the dog missed everything the certified dogs found and she was OK with that. Honestly, what an idiot!

Confession 9: Hiring the right company

In my years of experience with bed bugs this is what I have found to be the best and most effective bed bug method. I am so sure I can fix our customers' bed bug issues that I give a guarantee providing I receive FULL cooperation. This is my personal feeling: **Why not provide a guarantee? I'm an expert, you are hiring me as an expert, and I am charging you as an expert. If that is the case, I am going to take control of your current situation and fix your issue.**

Now I am going to be honest here. We service a lot of low end apartments. Not low end as far as the building but low end as far as the tenants.

Some don't have bed frames, so the beds are directly on the floors. Some live in cramped conditions. They have too many people, too many things and just not enough space. Some are just pigs and leave their crap everywhere.

In these types of conditions I will not guarantee our services. I will sell them -X- amount of services and if they need more it will cost them additional money.

Our methodology

1. I discuss with the owners or renters what is expected from them as far as properly preparing. I must receive the cooperation I am after (it doesn't work 100 percent of the time, but we get close)

2. I inform them this process requires several steps (if using conventional treatment methods) and may take a few visits before we achieve success. I tell them not to panic and I remind them that it is a process.

3. I always schedule two technicians for the initial treatment. This is the key to our success because we are turning over furniture and moving furniture around as part of the treatment. I need to make sure no stone goes unturned, and one technician isn't going to be able to do what is needed.

4. Once we start, we are going to use a variety of methods, such as vacuuming under the carpets and the beds. We remove all the electric outlet covers to inject pesticide dust. We apply residual pesticides to the furniture, floors, wall voids, molding, etc.

5. All of our jobs require the purchase of Protect-A-Bed mattress and box- spring encasement covers. These covers have been entomologist-tested and approved. You cannot buy these covers in the stores. They can be purchased for our web store at http://www.bedbugkillers.com

> **Do yourself a favor and don't leave your bed bug infestation to a company or person offering you cheap services. If never turns out good for you!**

It must be handled professionally by a certified technician who has bed bug experience. I have assembled a list of questions you can use to judge. I list these same questions on my website. I have been told by people all over the country who have visited my website that the questions saved them hundreds of dollars and hours of wasted time.

Please take advantage of my experience by letting my more than 25 years of pest services work for you.

Here we pulled off all of the radiator covers in every room in this apartment to seek out bed bugs. Thoroughness is definitely the key to a proper treatment.

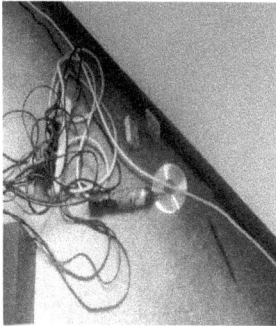

Finding Bed Bugs is an art! We leave no stone unturned. We pull apart everything we can in search of Bed Bug infestations.

We found bed bugs in an electric outlet cover in one of the bedrooms. The guy in this bedroom hardly stays here. The guy in the other bedroom is getting bit regularly. It's common for us to find bed bugs in sockets.

Another tenant not prepared. Now, if your closest looks anything like this, then you can't expect to get great results, even if we use heat or other conventional methods to eliminate bed bugs!

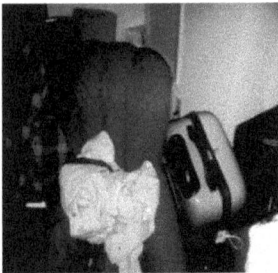

Here's another example of someone who wasn't prepared for us to inspect their apartment. I don't get the mentality of these people.

Estimates vs. Inspections

Free vs. Fee
Most people get confused. A free estimate is when a technician walks around your house for 10 minutes and gives you a quote. This is a free service. When we get called in for a possible bed bug infestation, what the customer needs is a

proper inspection and not just a price quote. A bed bug inspection takes time and experience, and I charge between $75 and $150 for it. Why on Earth would I spend an hour of my time for nothing? Try meeting with a lawyer or accountant for free for an hour — it isn't going to happen. If we do find bed bugs on our inspection we will either waive the inspection fee or discount it. In all my years of experience, people understand and respect the skill, so they pay. If they don't want to pay, then we send them elsewhere. Our goal is to give you great service and solve your current issue. In some cases our inspection reveals bed bugs aren't the problem, something else is. We then handle that something else.

Again I am going to EMPHASIZE: **Cheap services are expensive and expensive services are cheap.**

Questions to ask pest companies prior to hiring them:

1. Ask about the type of service they offer for bed bugs and if they have done these services before. If they say they treat one time and offer a warranty, forget it. One-time treatments may not work.

2. Find out if the person, not just the company, is a licensed professional or if he or she working under the license of the company. Remember the company you hire is only as good as the service technicians they send out to your home. **Ask to see their license.**

3. Ask about their follow-up procedures. What happens if the problem is not corrected or if you need additional services? Make sure you have **everything in writing**. Some companies will charge you an initial fee with some visits attached. After the allotted visits, they then charge per visit as needed. So let's say you continue to pay them because your bed bug issue has not been resolved. At what point do you say, "Forget about it. I cannot afford this anymore?" And now you are still left with bed bugs.

4. Ask how quickly they will come back out if you need additional services. You want to make sure they are properly staffed and organized so you don't have to wait more than 24 hours after you call. Who needs a company telling you they can't come till next week?

5. Ask if they have testimonials from satisfied customers. While it may not be company policy to hand out telephone numbers, satisfied customers are always eager to write good remarks.

6. Ask about weekend service. What is their response procedure if you have an outbreak on a Saturday or Sunday? While a lot of companies promise "24-hour service," off hours is usually answered by an answering machine. Therefore, it's not true 24-hour service.

7. Ask if they belong to any professional associations. You want to deal with an exterminator who is committed to keeping up with the latest trends and information about the industry.

The best way to initially start is by calling around. See who answers the phones or how quickly you are called back. Call on a Saturday afternoon or a Sunday. This is a good way to gauge the services a company is going to provide.

More Frequently Asked Questions

What recourse do I have as a consumer if I have had a bad experience with a bed bug exterminator?

Depending on your problem, you can contact the appropriate enforcement agency for your state. If the chemicals were not applied correctly, you can contact the Pesticide Control Program, if you're a New Jersey resident. In New York, contact the Department of Environmental Conservation (DEC). You can find out if the company is even licensed and if the company has had other issues with customer complaints.

What are some of the frustrations that people have experienced working with bed bug exterminators?

Great question. Actually, the majority of the frustrations that people have with bed bug exterminators are their own fault. A lot of consumers have this mentality that they shouldn't have to pay for professional bed bug exterminator services. They are looking for the cheapest price out there. When you have that mentality, cheap is always going to find CHEAP. Quality services cost money.

I, for example, have just as much knowledge about my industry as a doctor or lawyer has about theirs. If you wouldn't expect to go see a doctor or lawyer for free services, then you shouldn't expect to get free services from a professional bed bug exterminator either. As a consumer, you also need to ask the right questions when going through the process of hiring a bed bug exterminator. The better the questions you ask, the better the results you are going to get in selecting a good company and the services that they provide.

How do I know if I'm an idiot?
I'll bet you're wondering what this question has to do with bed bugs.

Well, it's when you start taking advice from friends, family members, and associates on how to treat for bed bugs. The more advice you take from people, who know nothing about bed bugs and are eager to give opinions, the more likely you will rank very high on that scale.

Final Thoughts
Make sure you do your research before you hire a company. You don't want to hire a company who's going to send out summer help or some guy with a sprayer. Also make sure they have the proper insurance and licensing. A good company won't have anything to hide.

The reality is this: No bed bug exterminator has a 'secret sauce' that no one else has access to when it comes to killing bed bugs. In fact, bed bug technology has only started to receive funding within the last six years. People are still learning about these creatures. Unfortunately, there are some unscrupulous individuals out there who are giving false information just to make a buck.

For example, there is no product out there that stunts the growth of a bed bug or stops the production of eggs. It's been researched, but it hasn't been developed yet.

Here are some stains on a box-spring caused by bed bugs. As you can see in this picture, we noticed the infestation when we removed the box-spring cover.

This is the most common place we find bed bug infestations or at least the signs of bedbugs.

You don't have to throw out your box-spring.

If you notice this, you can purchase the correct covers here:

www.bedbugkillers.com

Confession 10: Prepping for Treatment

The success of your Bed Bug Treatments is going to depend on your willingness to cooperate.

You are going to have to do a lot of work. Sometimes it's going to feel overwhelming. I get it! But these are your bed bugs and quite honestly if you want them gone you are going to have to do the work.

Typical chemical preparation will be:

1. Removing all clutter from the closets, floors and under the beds.

2. Dry-cleaning, washing, drying all clothes and bagging them in clean bags. (Secret- you can put all clothes in dryer on high heat to kill all stages of bed bugs- including your dry-cleaning)

3. Remove all electric items from sockets so these areas can be accessed.

4. You may have to throw out heavily infested items.

Confession 11: What to Expect After You Receive Your Treatment

Depending upon the type of treatment you receive you will experience various outcomes over the next several days. Keep in mind, if you received chemicals, the bed bugs MUST touch the chemical to be effective. Give the chemicals time to work!! Here is a list of some of the outcomes. There may be more but this is the most common.

1. Small bed bugs active and found walking on your bed - use a tissue

2. Feeling itchy during the night. - it may be just in your mind, happens often.

3. Heavy smell of chemicals. - keep windows open, leave area.

4. Bed bugs walking across your floor - affected by chemicals, use vacuum.

For us, we return in 10 days. No matter how many times I tell our clients what they may encounter, they still call up if they see live bed bugs and ask if something can be done? My response is YES, something is being done, see you in 10 days.

Confession 12: Heath Care Workers and Health Care Agencies

Believe it or not, the following stories are true.

My buddy XXXXX mother lived in Point Pleasant and relies on health care workers to watch over her. The mother is not capable of going places on her own. She gets bed bugs all over the house. The health care workers brought them in. He got the agency to pay him the $2,000.

Another customer calls me. His mother lives in East Brunswick, N.J., and is bedridden. The health care worker calls the woman's son and says, "We have animals in the house." The son says go get a can of roach spray, thinking ants or roaches are causing the problem. The mother is on dialysis and cannot speak. He sends me over to inspect. I find thousands of bed bugs in the mother's bed and in the health care worker's room.

In this scenario, some people call me up because they heard about me. Their mother is getting rashes and they don't know from what. They send me to inspect. It's a nicely kept apartment, but when I pull their mother's bed away from the wall, I find one of the worst bed bug infestations I have ever seen. The ONLY people besides her kids visiting her are the health care workers.

Listen, I'm not saying this will happen every time, but you have to be aware it can happen some of the time. Do your homework!!

If you need to hire a home care attendant I suggest you implement the following:

1. When dealing with an agency, let them know your feelings about this.

2. Talk to the home care attendant prior to hire. Ask her if she knows what a bed bug is and ask her outright if she has any.

3. Document each date, the name of the agency and person working.

4. Let the agency know that if ANY of its workers infest your residence, it's going to be held totally responsible.

5. If for any reason you start to notice a rash on your loved-one's body, take him/her to the doctor. Also inspect their bed for any evidence of a bed bug infestation and inspect the health care worker's bed too.

Look, I told you at the beginning that this was a no-holds-barred, straight talk book. You need to be aware of all possibilities.

Confession 13: Property Owner / Tenant Relationship

This is going to be an interesting chapter for you as the reader. I am going to give it to you straight: the good, the bad, and the ugly. I have updated this from Book l.

Over the last ten or so years, bed bug infestations have hit record numbers. Investors are overwhelmed and financially struggling because tenants refuse to take responsibility for their bed bug issues. Sometimes, tenants don't tell their landlord they have bed bugs and try to fix it themselves. Not only does this procedure not work, but in multiple-family buildings it makes the matter worse by causing the infestation to move into another apartment.

Some tenants move into the apartment bringing bed bugs with them and then blame the landlord. I actually see this quite often. I feel bad for investors, but hey I don't feel bad that they brought in the wrong tenant and now I'm going to take their money. Don't cry to me about you not making enough money. Totally NOT my concern.

Some landlords are scumbags and have no interest in fixing any pest issues. I did say "some," not all. Honestly, after seeing what I have seen, I do not blame them!

A lot of landlords I come across are just looking for a quick treat and paperwork to show the city officials. I am sure you will always find some unlicensed or low charging pest idiot to give you just that. Those mother fluckers have no right being in my industry.

Based upon my experience working with landlords and investors:

1. If an apartment has bed bugs and the tenant moves out, do the right thing and get the apartment properly treated. This is hard to do when you no longer have a host for the bed bugs to feed on. There are gadgets you can purchase that release carbon dioxide. Personally, we would bring in a K-9 team to make sure we achieved the results we were after.

2. When an existing tenant wants to move, have the apartment inspected by a qualified pest company to determine if this tenant has bed bugs and is not telling you. In some states you can charge the fees back to the tenant.

3. Before a new tenant moves in or you sign a lease, tell her she must get a letter from a pest control company saying that her old apartment has been inspected for bed bugs and none have been found. This needs to be an official letter.

4. When a tenant calls you up and complains about bed bugs, document it and take care of it. Do not advise the tenant to go to the store and spray them himself. This will only make matters worse and cause the infestation to spread.

5. There is going to be a cost factor. Spend the right money and get the job done correctly. Be a stand-up guy — a good tenant is worth their weight in gold. The landlords who use us are quite happy, and so are their tenants. We charge the right price to do the correct job.

You do not know how many calls my office receives from other tenants who find us on the internet. Instead of the tenant contacting the landlord or calling the pest company who treated them, they call us. By law, the tenant is required to receive a notice of what is being used. Personally, I don't get it. Good communication between pest control company and tenant makes for a happy relationship.

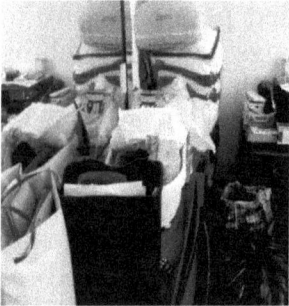

Here is a view of a tenant's apartment. The tenant was visited by us prior to service and given oral and written instructions. The tenant felt because she worked, she had no time to prepare. Even though she complained about having bed bugs.

I have personally come across so many tenants that have a bad attitude. They bring in the infestation, they live incorrectly, they don't want to cooperate, and then they call the local health department. It's a total victim mentality.

Here is another tenant's bedroom. This tenant is sleeping directly on the floor with this mattress. All the black you see is live bed bugs, Bed bug shit and bed bug eggs. We tossed this mattress off the 2nd floor terrace. The tenant was actually upset; he couldn't sleep in his room that night.

Here is a picture of another tenant not being properly prepared for an initial bed bug treatment. I swear you can't make this stuff up. for their issue even though **THEY CAUSED IT!**

This is in a boarding house we took over. All tenants were using these products in their rooms. NOT ONE (1) of these products worked for them. We removed over 30 cans of sprays.

Here's a can of bed bug spray next to a tenant's bed indicating they have a serious bed bug issue. The tenant told me he sprays himself and his bedding down each night prior to going to sleep. I am almost certain he got most of his furniture from the street.

I wish I could really say what I would like to. Thank G-D I was not raised by lowlifes.

The living conditions I see by some immigrants and poor uneducated people amazes me. To be honest, it's always the single guys or the baby mommas living this way.

As I wrap us this chapter I wish you as a landlord the best of luck! You need to screen and select the right tenants. You don't need to have trouble makers who take no responsibility for their current bed bug issues.

Confession 14: Bed Bug Legislation

There have been a number changes to legislation that have occurred throughout the country. On the state level, the vast majority of people are unaware of the new laws on the books, particularly renters and property owners.

Did you know in the State of New Jersey, that if you notice bed bugs in your unit, you are required by law to notify your property owner and that you may be responsible for the cost of exterminating those bed bugs in your unit if you fail to tell the owner or manager?

Another part of the legislation states that if you don't grant the landlord the right to access your apartment so the inspection and possible eradication of bed bugs can occur, including blocking access to allow for visual inspection, your landlord may not be responsible for damage or costs resulting from bed bugs.

A third provision allows landlords to deduct the cost of eradicating bed bugs from security deposits if the unit is deemed damaged because of their own negligence and the renter moves out.

Now, if you do your job and notify the landlord and they fail to act in 10 days, then you as a tenant can inform the local health board and they will inspect your unit. They can hire a pest company and recover the eradication fees from the landlord. In New York, property owners now have to notify potential tenants if they have treated or have bed bugs on premise.

Whatever state you currently reside, as a property owner or renter, it's critical that you educate yourself on your rights and your obligations so you can avoid heartache and fees.

Conclusion

So who can get bed bugs? Anyone! Make no mistake — bed bugs are not like other household pests and they can be challenging to eradicate. Female bed bugs lay up to 500 eggs in their lifetime, and these eggs hatch in 10 days.

These hitchhikers can gain access to your home, and you may not even know it. Bed bugs have been found in dressing rooms, taxis, buses, subways, planes, trains, five star hotels, movie theaters, restaurants, schools, and dormitories.

As you can see, bed bug infestations are at an all-time high and will continue to get worse. Most experts agree that this problem isn't going away anytime soon.

But here is the good news!

If you're faced with a bed bug problem and you are willing to use this book correctly, chances are you will be able to take the bite out of those bed bugs. You will also have the opportunity to save thousands of dollars and hours of frustration.

Now that you are equipped with the facts, you are ready to "BITE BACK!"

Share this Book with People You Care About, Help Me Help Them!

Empower and Equip Others!

Share This Book

How great would it be if you could help a friend, an associate or a loved one get through the trauma of Bed Bugs!

Now you can, with my book "Confessions of a Bed Bug Killer"

In this book, P Buggy reveals street strategies that are easy to understand and apply. The goal of this book is to teach you how to effectively keep bed bugs out of your life.

Special Quantity Discounts

1- 20 Books	$15.00
21-99 Books	$14.00
100—499 Books	$13.00
500-999 Books	$12.00
1000+ Books	$11.00

(These discounts are **ONLY** available Directly though my website. They are not available through Amazon)

Prices do not include shipping. Shipping is extra.

* When you hire P Buggy to speak at your event, it comes with 100 books you can hand out to your captive audience.

SCHEDULE SCOTT aka P BUGGY TO SPEAK AT YOUR EVENT

If you are interested in booking P Buggy to speak, you can contact him at his office in Edison, N.J. P Buggy is available to speak nationally and internationally.

To schedule call: 1-908-444-6097 in the USA

PBuggy@bedbugkillers.com

www.ingramcontent.com/pod-product-compliance
Lightning Source LLC
Chambersburg PA
CBHW060553100426
42742CB00013B/2536